Water Buffalo Days

Water Buffalo Days

Growing Up in Vietnam

by Huynh Quang Nhuong

pictures by Jean and Mou-sien Tseng

HarperCollins*Publishers*

Library of Congress Cataloging-in-Publication Data
Huynh, Quang Nhuong
  Water buffalo days : growing up in Vietnam / by Huynh Quang Nhuong;
pictures by Jean and Mou-sien Tseng.
      p.   cm.
  Summary: The author describes his close relationship to two water buffalo that were part of
his family when he was growing up in a village of the central highlands of Vietnam.
  ISBN 0-06-024957-9.
  1. Water buffalo—Vietnam—Central Highlands—Biography—Juvenile literature.
2. Huynh, Quang Nhuong—Juvenile literature. 3. Villages—Vietnam—Central Highlands—
Social life and customs—Juvenile literature. 4. Central Highlands (Vietnam)—Social life and
customs—Juvenile literature. [1. Water buffalo. 2. Huynh, Quang Nhuong. 3. Vietnam—
Social life and customs.] I. Tseng, Jean, ill. II. Tseng, Mou-sien, ill. III. Title.
SF401.W34H88 1997   96-35058
636.2'93—dc20   CIP
                                                                                     AC

Typography by Elynn Cohen
1   2   3   4   5   6   7   8   9   10
❖
First Edition

To my father
—HQN

Contents

Introduction

I was born in the central highlands of Vietnam in a small hamlet on a riverbank that had a deep jungle on one side and a chain of high mountains on the other. Across the river, rice fields stretched to the slopes of another chain of mountains.

There were fifty houses in our hamlet, scattered along the river or propped against the mountainsides. The houses were made of bamboo and covered with coconut leaves, and each was surrounded by a deep trench to protect it from wild animals or thieves. The only way to enter a house was to walk across a "monkey bridge"—a single bamboo stick that spanned the trench. At night we pulled the bridges into our houses and were safe.

There were no shops or marketplaces in our hamlet. If we needed supplies—medicine, cloth, soaps, or candles—we had to cross over the mountains and travel to a town nearby. We used the river mainly for traveling to distant hamlets, but it also provided us with plenty of fish.

During the six-month rainy season, nearly all of us helped plant and cultivate fields of rice, sweet potatoes, Indian mustard, eggplant, tomatoes, hot peppers, and corn. But during the dry season, we became hunters and turned to the jungle.

My father, like most of the villagers, was a farmer and a hunter, depending on the season. But he also had a college education, so in the evenings he helped to teach other children in our hamlet, for it was too small to afford a professional schoolteacher.

My mother managed the house, but during

the harvest season, she could be found in the field, helping my father get the crops home. As the wife of a hunter, she also knew how to dress and nurse a wound and took good care of her husband and his hunting dogs.

Like all farmers' children in the hamlet, I started working at the age of six. I helped look after the family herd of water buffaloes. Someone always had to be with the herd, because no matter how carefully water buffaloes were trained, they were always ready to nibble young rice plants when no one was looking.

Animals played a very large part in our lives. Many wild animals were to be feared. Tigers and panthers were dangerous and always trying to steal cattle. But a lone wild hog was even more dangerous than a tiger. The hog attacked every creature in sight, even when he had no need for food. The river held a different danger: crocodiles. Other animals provided food, labor, and often friendship. Watchdogs and water buffaloes were like members of our family.

I went to the lowlands to study for a while because I wanted to follow my father as a teacher when I grew up. I always planned to return to my hamlet to live the rest of my life there. But war disrupted my dreams. The land I love was lost to me forever.

These are my memories. . . .

Missing Water Jug

My family owned a small herd of water buffaloes, which consisted of two females and a male named Water Jug. The bull got his name because his big and round stomach resembled the kind of gourds we used as water jugs. Water Jug was a good worker and a good friend.

He had never been sick in his life, but when old age caught up with Water Jug, he died little by little, like a lamp burning its last drops of oil. For several weeks before his death he could not walk, and we had to bring food and water to him.

On the morning we found him lying dead, we buried him in the graveyard, as we had done for all the dead of our family.

Long after old Water Jug's death, I still missed him, and I often sat at his graveside remembering the good times we had spent together. During the rainy season, he had carried me on his back to the rice field, where I fished.

One day while sitting on his back and fishing for sword fish, I became restless. Normally the pond was full of sword fish, but that day I waited and waited and none of them would bite. I was making an earthworm jump on the surface of the pond to lure the fish, when suddenly I saw a huge, snakelike head shoot out of the water and snap at it. I was terrified and almost ordered Water Jug to back up and run. But soon the rest of a green turtle appeared and snapped the fishing line with a single stroke of her foreleg.

It took me a minute to recover, as I had thought the head belonged to a huge horse snake, the most savage reptile in the area. And at that moment old Water Jug lowered his head and snorted, ready to defend both of us.

I missed old Water Jug especially when it rained all day and frogs croaked loudly in the rice field. I wished I could go there on his back to catch those tasty amphibians. The two female water buffaloes we owned, like most water buffalo cows, were not trained to have people on their backs. And my parents would not let me go to the field alone, because they did not want me walking on all those slippery paths. So I had to stay home, listening to the endless croaking and missing old Water Jug more and more.

The Perfect Bull

When I learned that my father was determined to replace Water Jug with a strong male who could lead the whole herd of our hamlet, I was not enthusiastic at all.

Water Jug's hard work, patience, mild temper, and obedience had won the hearts of all the members of our family. I had hoped that my father would acquire another male as gentle and friendly as the late bull. I would not know what to do with a spirited fighter whose main function was to guard the whole hamlet's herd rather than to accompany me on various pleasant outings.

My distrust of belligerent males stemmed from my observation of the current leader of the herd, Hurricane. I once saw this fierce bull kill an upstart young male. With only the slightest provocation from the young bull, Hurricane had charged over and opened huge gashes in his stomach with his sharp horns. From that day forward, I refused to cross his path, even if I had to use another, much longer route home.

I did respect my father's dream of owning the most powerful bull, though, a dream that he had nursed since his boyhood. As a boy, my father had accompanied my grandfather to many distant places in search of a perfect fighter, but they had not found one.

Water buffalo experts told my father that the great bulls had in common these physical characteristics: Buffaloes with sturdy legs and thick necks were hard workers. Those with compact bodies could move faster during a fight, and ones with horns pointing slightly outward hooked their opponents more efficiently.

The experts told my father that the intelligence of a bull played a crucial role in his life as a fighter. There was a constant threat of tigers, panthers, and lone wild hogs from the nearby jungle.

My father dreamed of a bull that could be a valuable worker and a strong fighter at the same time. It was possible to have such a combination in an animal that had a fierce father from the mountains and a patient mother from the lowlands.

I did not wish for his failure, but I expected that the prospect of my future excursions in the field or woods would not be very bright if my father fulfilled his dream.

Bargaining

One afternoon during his patient quest for the perfect bull, my father came upon a powerful male guarding a herd on the slope of a high mountain. A thorough examination revealed to my father that the young leader possessed all the characteristics of a great fighter.

My father next approached the herdsman, who sat in the shade of a nearby tree. He asked about the owner of this magnificent bull and where he might acquire a young bull of the same quality.

It turned out that the bull's owner was Ong Kim, a former classmate of my father's. He told my father everything he wanted to know about the young bull.

Ong Kim had bought the bull two years earlier from a buffalo merchant who lived about twenty-four kilometers from his village. My father would have a very good chance of finding a fine bull at this merchant's ranch, for the trader always had on hand numerous males of various sizes and ages and from various sources.

On the way to the merchant's ranch, Ong Kim advised my father to be cagey while dealing with the cunning and greedy trader. If my father saw a buffalo he wanted to buy, he should not show any interest in that one. Instead, he should pretend to pay more attention to the others. In doing so, he might be able to beat down the price and get a good bargain for the buffalo he really wanted.

Upon arriving at the dealer's place, my father was very impressed by the number of water buffaloes available for sale. More than two hundred of them were scattered on a very well-kept ranch, surrounded by thick bamboo groves that made it impossible for buffalo thieves or dangerous wild beasts to penetrate the farm. A high fence, which separated the males from the females, prevented any disturbances caused by rivalry among amorous bulls.

Since my father planned to buy a young bull, he went quickly into the males' area. Ong Kim kept the merchant busy by asking him question after question in order to give my father enough time to carefully scrutinize each young male.

My father spotted a calf standing near a haystack. The yearling answered all his wishes. My father quickly moved away from his favorite and pretended to pay attention to another young male, a gray one. When the merchant and Ong Kim joined him, he said that he liked the bull, but he wished he were white, like the two females he already owned. The merchant then showed him all the white bulls he had, but my father politely told him that he did not like any of them.

My father walked back toward the gray

bull he pretended to like, and on the way he stopped by his favorite, who was still standing near the haystack. He asked the trader about the price of hay in the area, and about the amount of money spent to feed the herd, all the while nonchalantly patting the back of his chosen bull. During the conversation he glanced from time to time at the gray bull and repeated the same regret that he was not white. And then he said that he had made such a long trip to see the herd and that he hated to go home empty-handed.

While preparing to leave, my father turned around and looked at his favorite and casually asked the merchant: "How much do you want for this friendly one?" Seeing that my father was not eager buy any of his buffaloes, the dealer quoted a reasonable sum. My father then bargained with him for a while and finally bought the calf he wanted the most at a very good price.

On the way home, my father could not wait to show his family the magnificent calf. Ong Kim was very proud of my father's

negotiating skills, and he was also very pleased with the choice. He agreed with my father that the calf had mixed blood, half from the mountains and half from the lowlands. That was what my father had carefully looked for—the mixed qualities of a hard worker and an excellent fighter.

This calf could rise to a position of leadership. However, there was a crucial factor—intelligence—that remained to be seen. Without this quality, no matter how courageous, strong, and aggressive he was, the future leader could not last long.

The New Calf

At the gate of the merchant's ranch, the calf hesitated to go on. My father rubbed his neck, and Ong Kim gave him a handful of green grass he had just pulled from the edge of the rice field. The calf quickly changed his mind and willingly followed my father while munching the tender grass.

During the trip back to Ong Kim's home, my father led the young buffalo by a rope passed through his nose. Buffaloes' noses are quite sensitive, and a sharp tug on the rope would be very painful and would subdue the calf if he became agitated. Ong Kim walked behind, so he could push the calf in case he balked again. However, they did not have any trouble—the young bull followed my father obediently all the way back to Ong Kim's place. He behaved as if he had known my father for a long time. This pleased my father a great deal, because he had not expected the calf with the fierce blood of a bull of the mountains to obey his new owner so quickly.

It was late in the afternoon when Ong Kim's house came into sight. My father accepted his friend's invitation to stay overnight at his place, for it was too late to continue the trip home. To avoid a possible fight between my father's calf and the bull he owned, Ong Kim suggested that my father tie the young buffalo to a tree in the garden, far from the shed where Ong Kim locked his herd for the night.

My father was quite tired from the long journey, but instead of letting his friend's son feed the young bull, he did it himself in order to win the calf's trust. Before he went to bed, he returned to the garden to stay with the calf for a while longer. He wanted to strengthen the bond between them, and also to feast his eyes on his new possession.

Early the next morning, my father brought food and water to the calf again. Again he devoured the food and drank the water heartily. After eating, he showed great affection toward my father by licking his hand when he patted his head. When my father took leave of his friend, Ong Kim offered to accompany my father as far as he needed. My father thanked his friend but told him that he did not need his assistance, since the buffalo trusted him much more now.

After thanking Ong Kim once more for his hospitality and help in finding the calf, my father hurried home. He could not wait to show his family and neighbors his prize. The return journey seemed much longer to him.

As soon as my father arrived, neighbors crowded our courtyard, where the calf was temporarily tied to a stake. Buffalo experts

agreed among themselves that my father had made an excellent choice. An old man said that the physical characteristics of the calf reminded him of the greatest buffalo he had ever known. That bull had gone through many difficult fights without a loss. Finally he had died of old age, leaving behind many male offspring, but none of them had reached the greatness of their glorious father.

Many people gathered around the young buffalo, but he seemed very much at ease. He swung his tail from side to side and at times flicked his ears to chase flies away. The calf surprised everybody, because it was very rare to find a friendly mixed-blood youngster. He did not show any discomfort or nervousness when a neighbor raised one of his feet to examine a hoof. After careful observation, the man said that the narrow end of the hoof, its very flat bottom, and its relatively small size indicated that the calf had good reflexes. This quality would be essential during a fight against a quick and agile foe such as a tiger or panther.

When all the neighbors had gone home,

my father remained by the calf to watch him despite his long, tiring journey home. He was not tired of looking at the calf. He discussed with the family what our neighbor had just revealed—our young buffalo had good reflexes. He was very glad that all the experts admired the calf, but there was still one thing about the young buffalo that he was eager to know—his intelligence. My mother said that the calf did not look stupid to her and that she already liked him because of his friendliness.

Making Friends

I was six years old when my father brought the calf home. Watching the young buffalo, I knew he would become my good friend just as old Water Jug had been, and I intended to ask my parents to name him Water Jug II. My father's subsequent talks with his friends about the yearling's potential as a future leader of the herd did not worry me any longer. I thought that there was no way this friendly young buffalo would turn into a fierce animal like Hurricane. I firmly believed that I could touch the calf anytime I wanted to. If he let a neighbor raise his leg and examine his hoof, why not me, when I just wanted to pat his shoulder?

However, my father thought otherwise. He cautioned me not to come close to the young buffalo when nobody was around. In his presence he would let me give the young bull food and water, and sometimes let me touch his head. He explained to me that calves were unpredictable and that they obeyed anyone taller than themselves but did not respect children and sometimes hurt them.

My father added that since he did not know the new buffalo's reactions to children yet, it would be better for me to keep away from him when I was alone. I listened to my father, but my trust in the calf never diminished.

My father wanted my cousin, who was ten years older than I and caretaker of the family herd, to befriend the calf as soon as possible. My father advised my cousin to win over the young buffalo by treating him kindly and not imposing his will on him.

Each day my cousin fed him, and while the calf was eating, he scratched his neck or rubbed his shoulder. In the first few days he spent a great deal of time with the yearling, walking him about the hamlet and then in the field so that he could become familiar with the neighborhood. The calf needed to know the area well, or he might get lost if he became separated from the rest of the herd.

When my cousin led the calf along the numerous paths crisscrossing the rice field, he taught him not to eat the rice plants. Any time the calf showed a desire to eat the plants, he gently pulled him away from them and encouraged him to eat the green grass on the edges of the path. He repeated these lessons only a few times, and the calf left the rice plants alone. My father was very happy, because a slow-witted calf would not have responded to the training so well.

Despite the fact that the calf seemed happy at his new home, my father still kept the young bull tied to a tree in the garden. He was afraid that he might try to return to the merchant's ranch. Instead of being bothered by this lack of freedom, the year-ling seemed very much at ease. He spent time basking in the sun, rubbing his back against a tree, and from time to time bellowing at our two females to attract their attention. He seemed amused rather than disturbed by the quarrelsome chickens that often came to glean the few rice grains that dropped off the straw he ate.

There was a silly baby billy goat that often left his mother and explored the garden where we kept the young buffalo. He looked apprehensive when encountering the big newcomer for the first time. But soon he came closer to the calf when he realized that the big fellow meant no harm. Finally they became good friends, and the kid stayed with the calf more than with his mother.

Sometimes from my window I saw them sparring in the moonlight. The kid would make a friendly charge, then skip away play-fully while the calf remained in the same place, waiting for his friend to come back and butt him again. During the day, if the calf did not see his playmate, he bellowed a few times, and the goat would come. My father had intended to sell this goat because we already had a good billy goat. But he changed his mind when the calf and the goat became good friends.

Soon my cousin started training the yearling to allow a rider on his back. First he put a light object on the calf's back before heading out for the day. A few days later he replaced this object with a heavier one. When the young buffalo reacted favorably to this approach, he put me on his back instead of an object of the same weight. I was a little bit worried when the young bull stopped walking and looked back at me, but with my cousin's coaxing, he continued to walk around again.

My cousin told me to remain very still at first, and then to make calculated movements such as leaning forward, backward, and sideways or sliding down to the ground and climbing up on his back again. He told me to repeat these movements many times until the calf got completely used to having a rider on his back. Afterward he taught the calf how to turn left or right or to stop by pulling the rope through his nose. When the

calf responded well to all the training, he rewarded him with a piece of brown sugar, of which the calf was very fond.

Training a buffalo to carry a person on his back was essential, for the herdsman couldn't always follow his herd on foot through muddy fields or marshy areas. Besides, riding on a buffalo's back provided great comfort for a farmer after a long day of hard work in the field. The rider could lean forward and take a nap during the trip home, for buffaloes, once they know their way, can get home without any guidance. And during the rainy season, when each family's herd was in the field, someone had to ride on the back of a buffalo to keep the rest of the herd from eating the rice plants. No matter how well trained, some buffaloes always nipped at the rice plants if no one was looking.

When he accepted me as his rider, the friendship between the calf and me was begun. At each training session, my cousin advised me to pat the calf on the shoulder before climbing on his back, and then to repeat the same thing after dismounting.

Afterward he let me give the yearling the rewarding piece of brown sugar, which the calf always swallowed very quickly. Then he licked my hand for any traces of sugar still sticking to my palm.

One day while he was doing that, I dared to pull his head down and lean mine against it. The calf gently butted me on the forehead in a playful test of strength, as he had often done to his friend the billy goat. This reaction convinced me that the friendship between us had been firmly established. Soon after this, my father saw me pat the calf's nose without giving him any brown sugar, and the calf responding by licking my hand. From that time on, he decided, I could be alone with the young buffalo.

Exploring

Some of the best times of my life were spent roaming the rice field, riding on the young buffalo's back. I had ridden old Water Jug, but I had done so only when the old bull had not been needed in the field or at home. The calf's time was not yet in demand, so we were free to explore all the nooks and corners of the field or leisurely catch all kinds of living creatures for food or for fun.

One of my favorite pastimes was going after field crabs. The field was full of them, but they were hard to catch. They seldom ventured from their deep holes except at night. You had to stay very still near their nests and wait. When they came peeping out of their holes, you would hit them with a stick. But with the calf nearby making so much noise, eating watercress or green grass, no crabs would come to the surface. Instead, they would remain at the bottoms of their holes, about two or three meters down in the hard clay soil.

To solve the problem, I tied the calf to a very long rope and left him grazing far away from me while I was trying to ambush a crab. Field crabs tasted as good as sea crabs, or even better—especially at the end of the rainy season, when they had stuffed themselves in anticipation of spending the six-month dry season deep in their holes.

In addition to field crabs, land lobsters were very much sought after in our area. Land lobsters look like crawdads but are much bigger. They hid their nests in water plants, and it was almost impossible to detect them if you were walking on a path. But if you left the path and walked along beside it in the muddy water, you could find them easily. It was very tiring to walk in the mud, so I rode on the calf's back when I wanted to catch land lobsters. When I spotted a nest, I poured salt water into it, and the land lobsters jumped out like crazy. Quickly, I clamped a basket down over the nest so the lobsters couldn't escape into the water of the field. I always carried a basket, a bottle of salt water, and a bucket to hold the captured lobsters.

The young buffalo also helped me range far afield to capture fighting fish. The fighting fish in our region were so fierce and courageous that if we put two males into the same container, they would fight each other to the death unless we separated them.

The male fighting fish built his nest at the edge of a path and lived alone in it except for a brief time during the mating season. After mating, the male made bubbles that stuck together and floated on the surface of the nest. Each bubble contained an egg, and the male remained alone to guard the nest. He had to chase the female away to prevent her from eating all the babies hatching out of the eggs. The male always tried to hide the nest among water plants or grass, but with patience you could find it. When you discovered a nest, you used a basket to capture the male and put him in a container.

When the children in town saw me with a jar full of fighting fish, they were very excited. Fish from other areas could not defeat the ones I sold them unless they were much bigger. Some children did not have money to pay for a fish, so they would trade anything they owned—cookies, candies, or toys were welcome payment for me. I had sold fighting fish before, but my sales increased with the calf's help. Since I could catch more fish, I could afford to give away one or two now and then. When a boy lingered on and looked at my fish longingly, I knew that he had nothing to trade. I would give him a fish if he promised not to let the other boys know about it.

During the rainy season, the leaves of the golden water lilies growing in the rice field became very large, and many water birds used them as nests. The birds usually chose ponds far off the roads and in marshy areas to discourage people who might want to gather their eggs. They would even drop their eggs into the ponds if people approached their nests. Since the calf was very fond of water lilies, and I liked to have those eggs, we often went to the ponds together no matter how far away they were.

At first I watched the activities at various ponds while the calf grazed leisurely. If a bird kept coming back to the same pond, there had to be a nest there. Males always brought food to females sitting on nests. Then I would direct the calf toward that pond, and as I came closer, I would lie down on the calf's back. Water birds did not worry when water buffaloes wandered close to their nests. But if they saw me, they would drop the eggs into the water before I could even spot the nest. Sometimes I was lucky and could bring home several dozen eggs of different colors. As for the calf, his stomach would be so full of water lilies that he did not need any more food in the evening.

During the dry season, fighting crickets hid in holes or cracks deep in the hard clay soil of the rice field. Since their nests were very deep, the only way to capture them alive was to pour water into their holes. It was not difficult to discover a cricket's hiding place, but the problem lay in having enough water to pour in so that the suffocated cricket would come out of his hole. With the calf's help I could carry more water to the field and catch more crickets to sell to the children in town.

Most children bought crickets to hear them sing or to let them fight against other crickets. Crickets, unlike fighting fish, rarely fought to the death. They made a great deal of noise before they engaged in combat, but most of the fights did not last long. After the defeat of his cricket, the owner would pull a hair from his head, tie one end to the cricket's neck, and hold the other end and swing the cricket in the air for a while to make him angry. When he became really angry, then he would fight again.

I saw many fights, but only once did I see two crickets fight to the death. They were both golden, and each of them belonged to a friend of mine. I never forgot the day those two crickets fought. They were almost the same size, and when my two friends put them together in a box, they squared off immediately. Unlike other crickets, they did not sing fighting songs before they fought.

At first they opened their jaws, and each charged the other head-on in order to overturn his opponent. When neither of them could gain any significant ground, each grabbed the other and bit his adversary's legs off. After a while neither one had any legs left, and their wings were all battered and torn. Despite the fact that they both had numerous wounds, they continued squirming around and trying to bite each other's bodies. In the end one died, but the other still bit hard into his abdomen and refused to let go even when the owner wanted to separate them. About five minutes later, the victorious cricket also died.

A male cricket could sing three kinds of songs. The fighting song before a fight against another male was very frantic and shrill. The courting song was soft and insistent so as to attract the attention of a female somewhere nearby. But the night song was the best because of its melody and soothing effect. Sometimes it also seemed sad, because it reminded me of the loneliness of the night in the field.

Playtime

When the sun was hot, I usually stayed in the shade of a tree while the calf wallowed in the mud nearby. He liked mud very much, but any time I left the shade to do something, he got up and followed me. One day while he was immersed in mud except for his nose, eyes, and ears, I climbed up a tamarind tree to pick the fruit for my mother. Suddenly I heard the calf bellow. When I peered through an opening in the branches, I saw him nervously looking for me. I immediately got down from the tree, and he ran to meet me. He licked my head and shoulders and proceeded to get me all muddy.

After that day I often played hide-and-seek with the calf. When I saw the yearling was busy eating, I slipped behind a bush and waited for him to look for me. I then yelled and waved at him to let him know where I was. When he saw and ran toward me, I sneaked to another bush and let him search for me for a while at my former place. When I noticed that he became worried, I yelled and waved at him again. The game continued until I got tired, and then I let the calf find me. He became very happy, swung his tail from side to side, and butted me playfully on the head.

One late afternoon while the calf was grazing peacefully nearby, I leaned against a tree and dozed off under its cool shade. Suddenly I woke up and found the calf in front of me, nudging my side with his muzzle. At first I did not know what he wanted. I stood up, rubbed my eyes, looked around, and realized that it had gotten late and the sun had already disappeared behind the chain of mountains beyond the river. The calf was right: It was time to go home.

Sometimes, when I did not want to do anything in particular, I would just stretch myself on the calf's back and let him carry me where he liked. I gazed at the sky and forgot everything around me. I felt as if the sky moved, but not the calf and I. One day while doing this I suddenly fell into a pond full of water lilies. The calf was so fond of lilies that he jumped into the water right behind me.

Often on the way home, I would lean forward, hold the calf's shoulders in my arms, and close my eyes to rest. And often the monotonous movements of the calf would lull me to sleep. One evening I did not wake up even when the calf crossed the gate to our house. My parents panicked when they saw me in this prostrate state, and were quite relieved when they found out there was nothing wrong with me.

Sometimes instead of going to the field, the calf and I stayed in the garden, and the goat joined us. The billy goat had grown big and become cocky. Occasionally he and the calf still played together, but the game often turned into a fight. The goat always tried to bully the calf by butting him very hard. Most of the time I had to separate them so the goat would not get hurt.

One afternoon I left them alone while I went inside for a drink of water. When I got back to the garden, I saw the goat struggling to remain afloat in the pond. Immediately I called my mother for help, and we fished him out of the pond. After that the goat never went near the calf again, and they stopped being good friends.

Our two buffalo cows ignored the calf, because he was too young and small for them. As for the calf, he stopped trying to get their attention, since he had me as a friend.

The calf and I had other children of the hamlet as playmates. During the harvest season, some crops were ready to be harvested before the others. To avoid damage from rodents and birds, everyone in the hamlet helped each family store their grains as soon as possible, the men in the field and the women at home. On the nights when the other women came to our house to help my mother clean the grains for storage in the granary, they brought their children with them.

While the mothers were working in the lighted courtyard, their children and I played with the calf. The calf became a bus, and I was the bus driver. The bus route passed through the garden, the gate, and the edge of the banana grove. There were two bus stops, one at the gate and the other in the garden. We adorned the yearling with an old hat, hung a bell around his neck, and tied three red balloons to his tail. A long string was tied to the bell so that I could ring it from the calf's back.

When everything was ready, the passengers dispersed to the two bus stops, waiting for the bus to come. I climbed on the calf's back, rang the bell, and went to the first bus stop in the garden to pick up the first two passengers. After that I went to the second bus stop, let the first passengers get off the bus, and stayed there long enough so two new passengers could get on the bus. On the

first two trips I had to signal the calf to stop
at each bus stop, but on the third trip he
knew how to play and stopped by himself
when he saw the children wave. I needed
only to signal him to start again when the
exchange of passengers was complete. After
several trips, I stopped the calf near the
place where my mother and her friends were
working, gave him a piece of brown sugar,
and made him lie down to rest for a while.

While the calf rested, we transformed his

back into a table by covering it with green banana leaves. On this improvised table, I served my friends steamed ears of corn and sweet potatoes. The calf remained very still while we ate, but once in a while he would raise his head slightly to look back to see what we were doing.

When we had finished all the food, we decided that the calf needed a medical examination, because he had worked hard to carry us around. We took the old hat off the calf's head, untied the bell, and detached the three balloons from his tail. We then listened to his heartbeat, examined his tongue and teeth, and looked into his eyes and ears. One young doctor even pulled the calf's tail to make sure that it was securely attached. After our thorough examination, we all agreed that the calf was very healthy but very dirty. We drew water from the well and washed the calf all over. When we finished, it was late in the night, and all the doctors and bus washers followed their mothers home.

Naming the Bull

Whent the calf grew into a young bull, he spent most of his time with my cousin in the field. He tilled the land and brought the crops home. He drew water from the well, carried firewood home from the forest, and brought farm products to the marketplace. He worked with my cousin as hard as he had played with me. When the dry season returned, I loved having the bull to myself again. However, my father told me that he should go to the pasture with the other buffaloes in order to learn from the current dominant male, Hurricane, how to protect the herd from wild beasts. He insisted on this idea because the young bull had shown time after time the most crucial characteristic of a good leader—intelligence.

As time passed, our buffalo grew. Judging from his great size and strength, most of the inhabitants of our hamlet predicted that sooner or later there would be a fight for supremacy between our buffalo and Hurricane. So far our young male had not made any serious move to challenge the older bull. However, the herdsman noticed that while in the pasture, our bull often stopped eating and watched the leader from a distance.

At home, the young bull was still my best friend, and his affection for me seemed only to grow. But he had lost his carefree attitude, even though he was only three years old. During our time together in the garden, he no longer playfully butted me and then skipped away joyfully to avoid my make-believe blows. Nor did he chase after me cheerfully when I gave him a little kick in the leg. Instead, he walked around gravely or lay down for hours without showing interest in anything. However, once in a while he nudged his muzzle against my side or licked my face when I patted his head.

At first I was surprised by the gravity of the young bull, and I was not happy with this new behavior. When I talked to my father about it, he explained that the bull had reached maturity even though he was only three years old. He said that the bull was now like a young man, and that his behavior was normal since a young man did not play like a child anymore.

Even with this explanation, I didn't fully understand until one day when I held the bull's neck in my arms and found I could no longer reach all the way around it. For the first time, I realized that the bull had grown incredibly large, and yet he remained as gentle and obedient as if he were still a calf.

Our full-fledged bull did not have a proper name yet. My father wanted to determine his most important characteristic and give him a name that would be appropriate. For this we had to wait until the fight between our bull and the dominant male of our hamlet—a brutal fight that I never wanted or expected from my gentle, friendly giant.

One morning near the end of the rainy season, when our young bull left the herd and grazed alone, people knew that the fight between the two bulls was imminent. With each passing day, the tension between the two males had increased. Since O Lim, Hurricane's owner, was a good friend of our family's, my father invited him to our house to find a way to avoid the fight, which might result in the death of one opponent—or worse, of both of them. During the discussion, they agreed that there was no way to prevent the encounter. However, they could make the clash less damaging by blunting the tips of the horns of the two buffaloes with old rags.

So far the two adversaries had shown their animosity by facing each other from a distance and roaring. But one afternoon the tension reached its breaking point when a few young females left the older bull and joined the younger male. Immediately, Hurricane left the remaining herd and moved toward the newly formed group while bellowing so loudly that everyone in the hamlet went to the field to see what was going on. We chose a high ground to watch the fight that we could not prevent.

Our young challenger left his small group and faced the older bull with determination. The two bulls ceased to roar but kept walking toward each other. They stopped and positioned themselves when there were about fifty meters between them. My father told me that they were preparing to charge, and that the result of the head-on rush would tell which bull was stronger, since usually the weaker bull would fall backward.

Suddenly the two bulls ran at each other with all their force. We heard a mighty thud when their heads crashed against each other. Hurricane seemed a bit shaken by the shock. Although he did not fall backward, his forelegs buckled and his knees almost touched the ground. However, he quickly recovered from this disadvantageous position.

In the beginning, the fight was fairly

even. Each bull managed to deal the other forceful blows to the neck and shoulders, but since the tips of their horns were covered with rags, they did little damage to each other. Then they changed tactics by circling each other. This strategy is used for trying to overturn one's opponent with a sudden thrust. Once a buffalo is on his back, his opponent can easily kill him by opening his abdomen with a deadly hook to the body.

As the circling technique, followed by a sudden charge, proved to be fruitless,

the two adversaries resorted to pushing. Hurricane continued to fight well, but he was breathing harder and harder, and then he began to foam at the mouth. At this moment my father told O Lim that he would like to separate them. O Lim conceded that his buffalo was losing the fight, but said that to separate them now would not do any good. They would only fight again the next day. He felt it would be better to let them fight to the end so that one could establish definite supremacy over the other, and afterward they could live in peace with each other.

While my father and his friend were discussing the situation, Hurricane was losing ground. Suddenly the younger bull pushed him over a small dike. But once Hurricane was behind the dike, he was able defend himself much better. In this position neither bull could pull or push the other. So they locked horns and tried to break each other's necks. In his fury, Hurricane accidentally hooked his horns deep in the dike and pulled against it blindly. With one desperate jerk of his head, his horns tore away from his skull and remained half buried in the dike.

Everyone cried out with astonishment and pity at this sudden tragic turn of events. Hurricane was stunned, and blood streamed down his forehead. My father and my cousin rushed to our bull's side and tried to appease him in order to save Hurricane. They led the furious young bull away while O Lim, helped by other villagers, tried to stop the old bull's bleeding, using his shirt as a bandage. But the situation was hopeless. When he reached home, Hurricane collapsed and remained unconscious until he died about an hour later.

My father went to see O Lim that evening and told his friend that he was sorry about the outcome of the fight. O Lim begged him not to worry—no one could have predicted such a disaster. Besides, he was thankful to my father for wanting to separate the two furious bulls when Hurricane was losing. He told my father that he would let everybody know that it was he who had decided to let the fight continue. Afterward, he even insisted that my father stay for dinner with his family. Later in the evening, when my father took leave of his friend, the two of them liked each other even more than before the fight between their buffaloes.

I was shocked and also worried by the tremendous force and fury that our bull had displayed during the fight. How could I ride on the back of this fearsome creature ever again? But my fears were dispelled at my first meeting with the young bull after the fight. He remained the same gentle giant, nudging his head against my side when I touched it.

The following day my father did not send our bull to the field as usual. Early in the morning he went to the shed to see whether the young bull showed any sign of fatigue. There were some bruises on his shoulders that needed some ointment, but overall the bull was in good shape after such a brutal fight. He did not show any weakness; instead, he ate and drank heartily.

On this day our young buffalo finally received his name: Tank. My father decided on Tank because when he hit Hurricane, the blow was like that of a tank. My father, my cousin, and I were so proud and fond of Tank that we spent most of our time that day watching him. Tank seemed to miss the field, but my father decided to keep him home all day, more for us to watch him than for him to rest. My father's dream had come true—to have a good worker and an excellent fighter in the same bull.

My father wished that my grandfather were still alive so that he could know the happiness of owning Tank. But he also asked my cousin and me not to speak too much about our bull, especially in the presence of

O Lim and his relatives, who had suffered the loss of Hurricane.

The next day when O Lim came to visit us, my father promised him that as soon as one of our buffalo cows had offspring from Tank, he would give him a male to replace Hurricane. O Lim was very happy about the promise and spent most of his visit watching Tank with great admiration while sipping rice wine with my father. He told my father that if need be, he would lend a hand in training Tank to fight raiding tigers or panthers.

He admitted that he was very sad to lose Hurricane, but nobody could have done anything to prevent the fight. The only way would have been to keep Hurricane at home all the time, but as he added: "What would be the use of a buffalo if he were always kept in a shed?" Besides, he reminded my father, Hurricane's death resulted from a self-inflicted wound. My father was very happy to have such an understanding friend in O Lim.

Leading the Herd

During the rainy season, water buffaloes could graze in the rice field thanks to good grass growing on many paths and water lilies thriving in the ponds. But during the dry season, the clay soil of the field got so tough that all the grass withered and the water-lily ponds dried up. Fortunately, a stretch of land near the edge of the jungle remained grassy even during the dry season. But when the herd grazed on that pasture, they were vulnerable to attacks by wild beasts if the dominant male failed to protect them.

The dry season began a few weeks after Tank had assumed the leadership of the herd. When he led the cattle to the pasture for the first time, all the other bulls showed absolute respect for him. If he happened to pass near them, they kept their heads very close to the ground. If for some reason he lingered by them for a while, they slowly moved away. Quarrels rarely broke out in his presence. Occasionally some females tried to attract his attention by rubbing their bodies against his. But most of the time he stayed apart from the rest of the herd and kept a wary eye on the jungle.

Once in a while, when a silly young calf left his mother's side and skipped toward the dangerous zone near the edge of the deep forest, Tank stopped him by uttering a few roars and then nudged him back to the herd. If two young bulls were testing their strength in a friendly way, Tank would let them do so. But if they seemed to really want to hurt each other, Tank would step in and reestablish order. In his presence, cows were also safe from being harassed by amorous young bulls. In the evening he stayed back for a while to guard the rear of the herd when it started for home.

Tank's performance pleased and impressed everybody. His success as the leader of the herd brought a new measure of respect and honor to my family. Other buffalo owners offered my father straw from their stocks. They knew that my father had to feed Tank late in the evening, so that the bull could spend all his time guarding the herd while in the pasture. My father thanked his friends and said that his stock of straw seemed to be enough for the family herd.

Some of the boys in my hamlet taunted me because I was weaker than they. One of them in particular would harass me when I was not with my cousin or Tank. I tried to fight back, but I lost. But when I rode on Tank's back, everybody, especially the boy who bullied me, left me alone. Tank would attack anyone at my order. According to his training, two taps on his shoulder meant "danger," and two taps followed by a push meant "attack."

He was immediately on guard when he received the two taps of warning. And he rushed forward to attack when he received two taps with a push.

Riding on Tank's back helped me avoid more than bullies. I could also avoid the village hunting dogs. The hunting dogs raised in our hamlet were so fierce and aggressive that just their looks gave me goose bumps. Each was so big and strong that he could easily defeat two ordinary dogs. Their masters always chained them to trees or kept them behind fences, but I still worried that they would break their chains or smash through the fences and get me. But on Tank's back, high above the ground, I did not care how threateningly they barked or how sharp and long their teeth were.

Tank remained the gentle friend and servant he had always been. When my mother and I went to town to sell the products of our farm, Tank was an enormous help. He could carry a heavy load of sweet potatoes, bananas, corn, eggs, ducks, and chickens, and he walked for hours without getting tired.

Tank had many friends in town, and as soon as my mother had sold all her goods and was ready to do errands, children would ask my permission to climb on Tank's back. As many as seven children could sit on his ample back at one time. When there was no more room on his back, some children would hang on to his tail and swing. Some little girls bent his head down to smooth his whiskers, while others combed the tuft of his tail. They often opened his mouth in order to see his teeth. They were fascinated that Tank, like all water buffaloes, had teeth only in his lower jaw and no teeth at all in the upper jaw.

If very small children wanted to play, I would make Tank lie down. Little boys and little girls swarmed all over him. They sat on his horns, legs, shoulders, ribs, neck, and stomach. He remained very still while the children amused themselves, except for the occasional flick of an ear to chase flies away.

When my mother came back from her errands, Tank would be rewarded with a piece of brown sugar. Then he was loaded up again with me and a big basket full of

the things my mother had purchased. The children waved good-bye and repeatedly reminded my mother to bring Tank back the next time she came to town.

Even with Tank's new responsibilities, there was still often time for me to ride on his back and hunt wild game as we always had done. Near the end of the rainy season, we would go after wild chickens. Wild chickens lost most of their feathers at this time of the year and could not fly. They depended on their feet to escape from enemies, but they ran away only at the last moment. To hunt them, I sat on the back of my buffalo with a stick in my hand. Tank would carry me slowly among small bushes where wild chickens liked to hide. When a wild chicken started running away, I would throw the stick at her.

On Tank's large back, I could squat instead of sitting astride. This way, I could turn left or right quickly and strike at the fleeing fowl in many different directions. Tank learned his role very quickly. After only a couple of outings, he knew to abandon open places and moved from one bush to another to flush out the hiding chickens.

Sometimes I could bring home three or four wild chickens at the end of an outing. For some reason their meat tasted better than the ones we raised at home. Perhaps it was because they were very well fed at the end of the rainy season. Or perhaps they got more exercise than domestic chickens. Or maybe it was simply that I had caught them myself, with Tank.

In one outing a frightened chicken fled just ahead of Tank. I hurriedly threw the stick after her and accidentally hit Tank's left horn very hard. Startled, he stopped and looked back at me with a puzzled look in his eyes. At once I slid down to the ground, held his head in my arms, and patted his neck to let him know that I was sorry. Tank seemed to understand that I had not meant to hurt him and licked my hands in return. I never again threw my stick at a chicken fleeing in front of Tank, for fear of hurting him a second time.

Earthquake

D omestic animals living very close to the jungle often preserve their natural instincts. Most of the time our animals felt rather than saw danger and often warned us of the presence of enemies.

One afternoon we were not out in the field working because of the Lunar New Year holiday. The sky above our hamlet was clear, but the atmosphere became very heavy. Tank and our other buffaloes remained in the shed, eating. Suddenly they stamped their feet very hard and bellowed fearfully. We looked around and saw chickens and ducks run into bamboo bushes to hide, and in the ponds, fish of all sizes jumped frantically as if they were caught in a net. Our watchdog crawled under a bed and whined.

We quickly opened the door of the shed and let Tank and the other buffaloes out. At first Tank led his small herd to the garden; then he changed his mind and moved them to the banana grove behind the house. We then ran to the bomb shelter, and the watchdog followed us. About three minutes later a powerful earthquake shook the whole area.

The deafening noise made by trees falling, rocks crashing down from the mountains, and houses collapsing was terrifying. When it was over and we emerged from our shelter, we saw that both the house and the shed were demolished. Most of the fruit trees in the garden were either broken or uprooted by fallen boulders. We realized that if Tank and the other buffaloes had stayed in the garden, they could easily have been killed, because five of our eight huge mango trees had been knocked down. All the houses on the southern side of the hamlet were gone, but nobody got hurt. The casualties were limited to a few cattle that had been crushed by falling rocks.

That evening we cleared part of the garden of broken branches to make a place for our family and cattle to spend the night. It was relatively safe for us and for them to be in the garden, because a thick hedge surrounded it. Earthquakes like this one had struck our village before. But after those disasters, people had not built shelters for themselves or their domestic animals. Then wild beasts, attracted by the smell of unburied dead animals, had come to the hamlet and caused much damage.

While my father and my cousin barricaded the entrance of the garden with broken branches, my mother and I built a bonfire. The fire would help keep predators

away and at the same time keep us warm—
all our blankets were buried under heavy
debris. There wasn't much space in the garden. We were hemmed in by enormous fallen
trees, three water buffaloes, five goats, and
a watchdog. There would also have been
several hogs, but they determinedly made
holes in the hedge and went back to their
half-demolished sty.

This was the first time I had slept in the
open air, and despite the circumstances, I
thoroughly enjoyed it. Tank and the other
domestic animals, unlike wild beasts, liked
the fire very much. They lay down as close
as possible to it and stayed awake, while we
people tried to sleep to escape the terrible
day. But worry kept us wakeful, so my father,
my mother, and my cousin sat up near the fire
and talked about what they would do in the
next few days. While they discussed how to
build a new house and where to get the money
to finance their project, I stayed with Tank.

I leaned against Tank's shoulder and
gazed into the sky to count the number of
giant fruit bats passing by. The warmth of his
shoulder, the regularity of his breathing, the

beat of his heart, and the enormity of his body made me feel safe and comfortable. The lonely calls of nocturnal birds, the occasional roaring of tigers in the nearby jungle—these belonged to the insecure and unpredictable dark world outside our garden. Little by little I drifted into a gentle sleep.

Crocodile Alert

Late in the summer, when work was not demanding, my friends and I would sometimes give the herdsman a day off. When we crossed the river in front of our hamlet to get to an island to pick mangoes, we would bring the buffaloes with us. We could have reached the island by small boats, but we always went by buffalo because there was a good meadow on the island where our herd could spend the rest of the day grazing.

In order to safely cross the river with buffaloes, at least three strong boys would carry long lances made of ironwood. One boy would lead the herd and protect the front. The other two would each protect a side of the herd. Each guard held a lance in one hand and hung on to the tail of a buffalo with the other, letting him carry him along. This gave the guards better balance in the water, so if a crocodile attacked the herd, the guard would be better able to use the lance to scare him away or, if possible, to kill the beast.

The danger was limited, since crocodiles are very territorial and only a couple or a lone male would occupy a given stretch of the river. So no more than two crocodiles would be likely to attack the herd at one time. The guards used lances instead of hunting knives because sometimes a very intelligent crocodile would sneak below the surface of the river and try to pull either a guard or a buffalo down. If a crocodile did this, a lance was much easier to use in the water than a knife. In such a crossing, a small boy like me stayed inside the herd, grabbed the tail of a buffalo, and let the buffalo carry him to the island.

One morning while we were preparing to cross the river, Tank looked very uneasy. When we were ready, he refused to step into the water. Since the leader refused to go, the rest of the herd refused also. We were surprised and sensed that something was wrong. We searched the riverbank, and before long, a young boy detected the muzzle of a crocodile among the water plants floating near the shore. At once the boys threw their lances.

Suddenly an enormous crocodile, pierced by a lance, jumped into the air and fell back into the river with a huge splash. The beast disappeared in the disturbed water. But we still could see part of the lance, so we could track him as he rushed toward the middle of the river and then turned downstream. The next day people saw the giant crocodile floating in the river with the lance still in his back.

That day could have been fatal for one of us if Tank had not sensed the danger. There was always much confusion when the herd first entered the water. During this short time, the guards had not yet gotten into their positions, and they couldn't see clearly

because some buffaloes preferred to jump into the river rather than walk in, and this sent up huge splashes of water. That intelligent crocodile must have noticed that we often used this place to cross the river.

It was fairly easy for the guards to protect the herd and defend themselves in the middle of the river. But when they were still at the riverbank, and they did not yet have a hold on a buffalo's tail, a crocodile making a surprise attack could easily pull one of them away into the deep waters and finish him off.

After this crossing incident, Tank won the hearts of all the people in our hamlet, young and old. Even the boy who used to bully me tried to make friends with me. A few days after the incident, he brought me cookies and asked if he could ride on Tank's back. I let him ride Tank, but I refused the cookies, which I suspected he had stolen. Afterward he admitted that he had swiped the cookies from his grandmother. When he left, he agreed with me that it would be better for him to return them to his grandmother. She was a very fierce woman.

A Fierce Fighter

Each buffalo owner in our hamlet chipped in to hire a herdsman, usually an old man who could no longer work in the field, to be with the herd in the pasture during the dry season. The herdsman's job was to alert people back home if there was a raid from a wild beast so that they could rush to the meadow to rescue the herd.

Early in the morning, he would ride the

buffalo he liked best as the herd made its way to the grazing area. He carried with him his lunch, enough water for the day, and a horn to blow in case of danger. Between the time the herdsman first blew on his horn and the arrival of the rescue party, it was up to the dominant male to hold off any attacker. Dominant males that were not alert enough or strong enough would lose their lives before the arrival of the hunters. Or sometimes the male leader was able to protect himself but not the rest of the herd, and a raider would make a killing and carry off a buffalo.

When Tank first assumed the leadership of the herd, my cousin trained him to fight against dangerous wild beasts such as tigers or panthers. With old linen and straw, he made a stuffed tiger and used it to simulate the attack of a big cat from various angles. Carefully, he taught Tank how to roll over and quickly get back on his feet if a big cat jumped on his back. A tiger or panther landing on a buffalo's back could attack the nerves centered around his shoulders and cause him to run into the jungle, where the big cat could more easily devour him. But a well-trained buffalo would make the cat jump away by rolling over.

Besides big cats, lone wild hogs posed the most serious threat to the cattle. A fully grown boar weighed between 225 and 275 kilograms, and most of his skin was covered by a thick coating of sap from a tree we called an oil tree. By instinct and sometimes because of the itch caused by parasites, the wild hog rubbed himself against the oil tree, which oozed sap profusely when its bark was broken. The sap condensed and dried on the boar's skin and was extremely tough to break through. And the coating only became thicker with age. The dried sap protected the animal with the efficiency of armor—a wild boar was almost invulnerable to knives or small firearms.

The only part of the wild hog's body that was not covered by this special sap was his throat and part of his neck below the ears. The hog rubbed the sap away from these areas so that he could move his head freely. The head of the hog had to be free from any hindrance, because it was the animal's most powerful weapon.

When a wild hog charged, he might knock his opponent down, but this alone would not inflict a deadly wound. It was the subsequent slap of the head that was fatal. The tusks of a wild hog curved out in such a way that a slap of the head could take away the whole abdomen of a pursuing hunting dog. With age the tusks turned inward, but when a wild hog was cornered, he would break his tusks by smashing them against a tree, and the remaining parts would point outward. Thus armed, the beast was prepared to fight to the death.

Wild hogs normally lived in groups, and each group had a dominant male. The dominant male was dangerous only when cornered by hunters and their dogs. But once in a while there was a lone wild hog—either one that was not strong enough to challenge the dominant male and preferred to live alone, or one that had been a dominant male himself but had been deposed by a younger, stronger rival. A frustrated lone wild hog was the most ferocious animal of the jungle. He might attack anyone or any animal in sight. Even a tiger would avoid a lone wild hog unless the big cat was very hungry.

Given this ferocity and determination, it was difficult to train Tank to take on a lone wild hog. But to make him a more formidable fighter, my cousin would attach a sturdy, razor-sharp knife to each of Tank's horns before letting him lead the herd to the pasture.

One day Tank's mettle was tested in a savage encounter with a lone wild hog. It was late afternoon when the herdsman saw that Tank was snorting and stamping his feet. He also noticed that the mature males and females had quickly formed a circle around their young. Minutes later, to the old man's horror, a huge wild hog came charging down the hill. Immediately the old man climbed up a tree and began blowing his horn wildly.

Tank rushed forward with his head very close to the ground and met the charging wild hog at the foot of the hill. A heavy thud rang out when their heads collided. The hog fell backward but got up quickly. Before he could position himself to deliver a slap of his head, Tank hooked him with a powerful blow to the ribs. The hog staggered sideways. The herds-man saw that the knife attached to Tank's left horn was broken in two, and half of its blade lay on the ground, glittering in the sun.

With any other animal, this blow could have torn open a rib cage, but the hog seemed unhurt thanks to his coating of sap. Recovering quickly from his second fall, the hog charged Tank again, and again the hog fell backward when their heads collided. When the hog tried to slap Tank for the second time, Tank hooked him with his right horn. This knocked the hog off his feet again, but also broke Tank's second knife.

After this fourth fall, the hog looked tired, but instead of breaking off the fight, he kept charging again and again. At one moment, Tank did not keep his head low enough to meet the hog's onslaught, and he almost reached Tank's front legs. If Tank fell, he would be dangerously vulnerable to a slap to the neck or abdomen. But luckily, Tank managed to stay on his feet.

By the time the first men of the rescue party came within sight of the battle, the hog had become tired, but he kept attacking. Finally, Tank met the hog's charge with his head almost touching the ground. He managed to pick up the hog with both horns and throw him over his shoulders. Unfortunately for the hog, he landed on the sharp angle of a rock and broke his back. Tank then turned around and started goring the wounded animal unmercifully. The hog could not move much anymore, but he still tried to slap back at Tank.

At last Tank caught the hog's throat with one horn. The hog tried to shake himself loose, but the more he shook, the deeper the horn sank. Finally, after a few desperate jerks of his chest, the hog succumbed to the fatal wound. At this moment the herdsman climbed down from the tree and loudly called Tank's name to stop him from goring the dead hog.

When the rescue party actually arrived on the scene, the men were very happy to see the dead hog. My father and my cousin examined Tank carefully, but they did not see any serious wounds. Tank had a few bumps and bruises on his head, near his ears, which only needed some ointment. All the blood that covered his forehead and neck came from the hog. The old herdsman asked my father if he could keep one of the broken knives as a souvenir of that unforgettable day.

The hog, which weighed almost 275 kilograms, by rights belonged to my family because Tank had killed him, but my father shared him with every family in the hamlet. He kept the two tusks, which were intact, and hung them around Tank's neck. When Tank shook his head, the two tusks struck against each other, producing light, high notes. These were cheerful sounds, especially at night, because they reminded us of Tank's presence, a thing that made us happy and proud.

Tank, I suppose, looked odd with his wild-hog-tusk necklace. It attracted great attention from travelers who passed through our hamlet. They were all amazed when they learned that Tank had defeated a lone wild hog. Some of them asked if they could see the skin of the hog, which we hung in the sitting room.

One traveler offered my father a great sum of money for Tank, but my father refused. He told him that Tank belonged to the whole hamlet, and he would not let his friends and neighbors down by selling him. Besides, my father added, Tank was like a member of the family to him. My father told the stranger where he had bought Tank, and said he hoped that he could find a similar buffalo at the merchant's ranch.

A few days later the same man came back and offered my father a much greater sum because he had not found a buffalo of the same quality. Again my father turned down his offer. When the stranger lingered on and tried to convince my father to put the rope back through Tank's nose, my father became suspicious about his motivation.

The man told my father that he had heard stories about buffaloes that had suddenly become unruly or raving mad because of some kind of disease. A strong bull like Tank would be very difficult to subdue if he became crazy, he said. My father told him that he had removed the rope in order to keep buffalo thieves away from Tank. He also mentioned how one thief had been badly hurt in his attempt to spirit Tank away. When my father finished the story, the stranger left and stopped bothering us.

When the children in the neighboring town saw Tank's necklace for the first time, they knew there must be a story to be told. But they could not believe their ears when they heard that Tank had killed a lone wild hog. They wondered how Tank, so gentle and friendly, could have done such a thing.

My mother explained to them that the hog had left Tank no other choice. He had attacked the herd without any provocation and without any need for food, since wild hogs are strictly vegetarian. As the leader of the herd, Tank had to fight the hog to protect the other buffaloes. Besides, if the hog had not been so stubborn and had broken off the fight when he had become very tired, Tank would not have killed him.

When my mother finished the story, a little girl came to Tank and held his head in her arms. She then told him that she did not know that he was so brave. Until then they had considered him a docile pet. The knowledge that Tank was not only a harmless giant but also a fierce fighter, a leader of the whole herd of the hamlet, filled their hearts with even more admiration for him.

Father and Son

When Tank was four years old, he had a son by one of our cows. In the evenings, when Tank had finished all the work that we asked of him, he spent time with his son, training the calf to fight. Tank would spar with the young bull, showing him how to charge, retreat, and circle the enemy. When the calf had horns that were long enough, he learned from his father how to deliver left and right

hooks. Sometimes when the moon was bright in the sky, Tank and his son kept practicing late into the night. They were quite noisy, and eventually my cousin or my father would have to go out and push both of them into the shed and shut the door so we could all get some sleep.

My father did not forget his promise to his friend O Lim that he could have the first of Tank's male offspring to replace Hurricane. He was only waiting until the calf was old enough to be separated from his parents. When this time came, he chose a day when Tank was not home and asked O Lim to come take the calf away. In the evening, when Tank came home, he desperately looked around for the calf, who had not greeted him as usual. He searched the shed, the garden, and the banana grove. He then went back to the rice field and roared loudly to call his son. He did not come home when it got dark outside.

That night Tank went to every house in the hamlet that had buffaloes. When he arrived at O Lim's home, he sensed that the calf was inside the shed. At first he walked around it to find an opening, but since he could not find one, he tried to demolish one of its walls. At this point O Lim sneaked out of his house and opened the door of the shed to free the calf. Tank brought his son home, and the rest of the night we heard him snorting at even the least suspicious noise.

Since promises between friends are sacred, my father decided to try again. As before, he gave the calf away when Tank was not home. This time O Lim blindfolded the calf and took him by boat to a friend's house about five kilometers down the river. That evening, when Tank came home, he became as desperate as the first time. He spent the night looking for his son in every shed of the hamlet. When the search proved fruitless, he disappeared at dawn.

All our family spent the whole morning looking for Tank, but we could not find him. In the afternoon O Lim's friend came to see him in a panic. He looked very scared and said that a huge water buffalo was at the monkey bridge in front of his house and threatened to charge anyone who wanted to cross. The wide and deep trench that surrounded the house on three sides prevented the buffalo from charging into the house. But the river, which limited access to the fourth side of the house, would be a problem. For the time being, the buffalo could not get across the river because of the deep mud on the riverbank. But in the evening, the water level in the river would rise, and the angry buffalo could easily swim across.

The friend had sneaked out of his house through the back door, gotten into a small boat, and rowed as fast as he could in order to find O Lim and let him know what was happening. Without losing any time, the two friends got into the boat and returned as quickly as they could to the scene, where Tank was still roaring furiously. Together they got the calf into the boat, rowed the boat away from the house, and then brought the calf ashore. When Tank saw his son, he ran straight to him. He licked the calf all over and then led him home.

When they arrived, the mother of the calf came out of the shed at once, leaving behind the food and drink we had just given her, to meet her son. She lowered her head and rubbed it against the calf's side. As for Tank, he was hungry and ate heartily. Perhaps Tank had not eaten all night and all day. Occasionally he raised his head and looked suspiciously in the direction of the gate of the house.

After this O Lim told us that he had decided not to take the calf, because there was no way for him to do so. He thanked my father many times for his efforts. Later on he told people that my father had kept his promise and that it was too bad that he could not accept the gift of the handsome calf. He also laughingly added that if he moved the calf to a remote place, the whole hamlet would lose Tank's service because the bull would leave the hamlet forever, in search of his lost son.

Hunting

One day one of our friends gave us a puppy to replace our watchdog, who had recently died of old age. We named the puppy Midnight because of her black hair. At first Midnight was very lonely, because she had no friends. If she came close to the rooster, he jumped on her and pecked her. When she wanted to play with the chicken brood, the mother hen chased her away. At that time we had a goat that had just had babies, but she too refused to adopt our new dog.

Finally we tried to make Tank and the puppy befriend each other, but we were not sure if Tank would like the newcomer. He had not gotten along very well with our old watchdog because the dog had become sullen and quarrelsome in his old age. But it was important to me for Tank and the puppy to become friends—I wanted to bring the dog along when Tank and I went hunting.

To our surprise, Tank accepted the puppy right away. The first time I brought the tiny dog to him, he pricked up his ears and looked at the small creature with curiosity. Then he reached out and licked the puppy soundly, and we knew that Tank and Midnight would be friends. Afterward I made Tank lie down so that the puppy could play with him. Tank lay on his side, stretched his neck, and playfully butted the apprehensive puppy. At first she whined, but little by little she became bolder and realized that the big fellow wouldn't do her any harm.

When Midnight was big enough, I started training her to be a game retriever. A good

retriever would save a hunter from being unnecessarily fatigued during a long hunting trip through the rice field or a marshy area. The hunter could remain comfortably on the buffalo's back, and the dog would fetch the game for him. I let Midnight ride on Tank's back with me, and then I trained her to jump to the ground to fetch a stick for me. Later I taught her not to move or bark when I was approaching one of the birds that greatly damaged the crops during the harvest season.

In our region, people used slingshots to scare the birds away or to shoot them down. Hunters liked to keep birds such as doves or wild ducks for their own tables. They sold the other birds to farmers, who would hang the dead birds in their fields to scare the other ones away.

Slingshots were very accurate if you used round clay balls as projectiles. However, you needed to get within twenty yards of your target in order to have a good shot. Birds were not afraid of cattle, and they even landed on buffaloes' backs to seek parasites. But if they saw a dog or a cat around, they flew away immediately. A game retriever had to know how to remain quiet and still when the buffalo was approaching the bird.

One day while hunting on the riverbank, I hit a bird with my slingshot and broke her wing. The bird fell into the river and tried to swim away. My retriever immediately jumped into the river to catch the wounded bird. Suddenly she howled in pain, and I saw that something beneath the surface of the river was trying to drag her down to the bottom. I quickly scrambled off Tank's back and jumped into the river to save Midnight. When I heard a big splash of water behind me, I looked back and saw Tank also in the water, a few meters behind me.

When I got close to Midnight, she suddenly stopped howling and swam easily. Right at that moment I felt a terrible pain in my left foot as some animal bit my toes and tried to pull me down. I used my free leg to stomp on the animal, but he only bit me harder. When Tank reached me, I grabbed his tail to steady myself. Then I raised my left foot so my free hand could grab the animal, who had sunk his teeth into my toes.

When I got hold of his neck and felt the furry skin, I knew it was an otter. He stopped biting and tried to get away from me, but I held firm. He thrashed and jerked and scratched me very hard, but I kept hold of him while Tank carried me back to the bank. When I got on dry land, I saw my toes were bleeding so badly that I had to use a clay mudpack to stop the blood. I was so angry at the otter that I planned my revenge all the way home.

When my mother saw me all wet and angry, with a strange patch of mud on my left foot and an otter pinned down on Tank's back, she hurried out of the house to help me get down. I hopped into the house with the otter in a viselike grip. With my mother's help, I tied the otter's legs as well as his muzzle—if I left his mouth free, he would chew through the string in a few seconds.

My mother calmly listened to my many plans for revenge while she cleaned and dressed my wound. She then called Midnight to her side and examined the dog's wound. The otter had bitten her left hind leg, but the wound was not deep and she had licked it dry. Midnight seemed angry at the otter too and growled at him menacingly.

Satisfied that we were both on the mend, my mother asked me what I had decided on as the otter's punishment. I told her that I would attach a string of firecrackers to his tail, untie the otter, and set the firecrackers on fire. My mother agreed in principle that the otter deserved punishment for his nasty behavior, but she thought that the firecrackers might burn the otter's tail. And, she added, the otter might have a heart attack and die. Thus the punishment seemed much more severe than the crime.

Suddenly I remembered how my cousin had caught a rat, attached a bell to his neck, and set him free in order to scare other rats away from the granary. My mother reminded me that the rat did scare all the other rats away, but he also drove our watchdog nearly mad and his barking had kept us awake many nights. Besides, she asked, what would be the purpose of hanging a bell around an otter's neck? I said that the bell would remind the otter not to be mean again.

When my father came home from the rice

field, he told me that I was lucky, because otters seldom lived alone like the one that had attacked Midnight and me. If it hadn't been for Tank's help, the otter could have hurt me more seriously and then gotten away.

My father made me promise not to let Midnight retrieve any more game falling into the river, because there were worse dangers there than otters. He smiled at my plan to hang a bell around the otter's neck, but he had another idea.

The next day my father put the wild otter in an iron cage and let our tame otter approach him. We kept a tame otter to catch fish for us, and my father hoped that the wild one could be similarly trained. But the wild otter kept turning around in the cage restlessly, and as soon as he saw the domestic otter, he showed his teeth angrily and scared the tame one away.

During the next few days my father tried to feed him with fresh fish caught by the other otter, but he refused to eat and remained sullen. Finally my father wanted me to free the wild otter without attaching any bell to his neck. I did as my father asked without bearing any grudge toward the crazy otter. My anger was gone, and the bites on my toes were healing.

Tiger Ambush

We often let Midnight follow the herd to the pasture during the dry season. The herdsman liked the idea because with her around, he felt less lonely. Besides, he could take a nap now and then in the shade of a tree and know that she would awake him in case of danger.

One morning in the late summer, when the herdsman, Midnight, Tank, and the rest of the herd arrived at the pasture, they noticed a heavy silence. There were no birds hopping on the ground or singing in the bushes, no squirrels running from tree to tree. The herd did not scatter across the meadow as usual, but remained in the same place while Tank snorted and scrutinized the edge of the jungle. Midnight did not play with the calves as usual, but walked around nervously, whining from time to time.

The herdsman considered taking the herd back to the hamlet but decided to let the buffaloes stay in the pasture for the rest of the day. He was afraid someone would say that he had become lazy and wanted an excuse to spend the day at home. He looked around carefully to make sure that Tank as well as the other buffaloes were far away from any thick bushes that could conceal a sudden assault. Then he called Tank and Midnight near him and picked the little dog up and put her on Tank's back.

He felt that in years past he had been a brave man. He had helped hunt down dangerous wild hogs and horse snakes that threatened the village. But now he had become too old to aid his two friends much in the event of an attack. With tears in his eyes, he patted Midnight's head and Tank's shoulder before climbing into a nearby tree.

Nothing stirred, and time passed slowly. Toward afternoon the old man dozed off in the tree, but he was suddenly awakened by the barking of the dog and the bellowing of the herd. The buffaloes had not bellowed during the attack of the lone wild hog a few months earlier—what could this mean?

Then, to the old man's horror, a huge tiger left a thick bush near the edge of the jungle and walked slowly toward the herd. Apparently the tiger had lain there in ambush for several hours, but the element of surprise had been lost because no buffalo had come near her. Finally she had decided to come forward and make an attack in the open.

Unlike the time he fought the lone wild hog, Tank did not come forward to meet the tiger halfway but remained where he was. He faced with determination the approach of this most formidable foe while Midnight, still on his back, barked furiously. The herdsman blew his horn frantically, and the herd formed a defensive circle around their young. The herdsman kept blowing his horn, but he knew that the fight would be short and savage. The clash would be decided by two or three moves from each adversary, and the encounter would be over long before any rescue party could arrive.

When the tiger came closer, Tank lowered his head and adopted a defensive position. Midnight ceased to bark and crouched on Tank's back, ready to assist. The tiger walked to and fro in front of Tank and Midnight and suddenly made a false charge, but Tank did not budge. The tiger then seemed to think better of tangling with Tank and Midnight and tried to circle around to the herd.

Tank abandoned his defensive stand and charged the big cat from behind. Midnight momentarily lost her balance and fell to the ground, but she jumped back on quickly. The tiger deftly avoided the attack and then turned around to face her opponents again. Tank again adopted a defensive posture while his foe started circling him, trying to find an opening.

Since Tank kept moving to face her,

the tiger finally made a decisive move by jumping right on Tank's lowered head. She succeeded in grabbing Tank's head, but when she struck, Tank hooked her in her left side, and the sharp knife attached to Tank's horn opened a gaping hole in the tiger's abdomen. Blood streamed from the wound, but the tiger firmly held on to Tank's horns and tried to bite into the top of his head. A well-placed bite on his forehead could penetrate Tank's skull and kill him instantly, but the tiger could not sink her teeth in because Tank shook his head so violently.

Midnight took this opportunity to jump from Tank's back and bite deeply into one of the tiger's hind legs. At that very moment, a young bull left his position in the protective circle and came forward to assist Tank. But before the young bull could get near, the tiger let go of Tank's head and turned to deal with Midnight by biting her shoulder.

When the tiger turned, Tank succeeded in goring her a second time, and in doing so he lifted both the tiger and Midnight into the air and threw them a few meters away. The tiger, unlike the stubborn wild hog, knew her

cause was lost. She broke off the fight and fled into the jungle. The young bull now saw his leader out of danger and returned to his position in the herd.

The herdsman climbed down the tree as quickly as he could to assess his friends' wounds. Despite the potentially fatal encounter, Tank had only a few scratches and bruises on his forehead and muzzle. However, the wound on Midnight's shoulder looked serious, and blood gushed out of it. The old man took off his shirt and tried to stop the bleeding.

Soon my father, my cousin, and the rest of the rescue party arrived on the scene. They attended to Tank and Midnight as best they could, and when Midnight seemed out of immediate danger, my father told my cousin to take Tank and her home. At first my cousin wanted to carry Midnight in his arms, but then he changed his mind and put her on Tank's back, and the three of them went home. When he saw Midnight shudder, he took off his shirt and covered her with it.

The herdsman had told the story of the fight about five times, but the rescue party did not tire of hearing it again and again.

They also wanted to know which young bull had attempted to assist his leader. When the old man identified the young buffalo, his owner was extremely pleased and proud.

Judging from the trail of blood the tiger had left behind, the men knew for certain that she was in serious trouble. It was necessary, however, to follow the tiger into the jungle and finish her off, or she might return to attack the hamlet in a wounded rage. Still, they did not unleash all their attack dogs, for fear that they might lose some of them to the wounded tiger. Too many dogs unleashed at the same time would only get in each other's way. There might not be enough space in the thick jungle to avoid the tiger's charge. The village chief decided that they should let loose only three hounds besides the lead dog. Then the men followed cautiously with the rest of the dogs on leashes.

After about a half hour, the frantic barking of the lead dog signaled that he had found the tiger. The men spread out so that no one would hinder another's strike with a hunting knife, but not so far apart that they would not be able to assist each other. The men and their dogs moved steadily forward in their new formation. They listened carefully, but to their surprise, there was no roaring of the tiger and no growling of the dogs, which would have indicated a fierce fight. Only the continuous but gradually less excited barking of the lead dog was heard.

When they came closer, they saw the tiger with her face half in the water of a small creek and the four unleashed dogs standing idle nearby. When they examined the dead tiger, they realized that it was the initial wound in her abdomen that had killed her. The knife attached to Tank's horn had slashed the tiger's stomach and liver. The tiger would also have died of the second wound alone, but she might have been able to survive that wound for a few days. Everybody agreed that Tank was a skillful fighter and that Midnight had played a crucial role during the encounter.

At first we feared that Midnight might die, but when my mother dressed her wound, she found that the injury was not as bad as it looked. After only a few days, all of Tank's wounds were healed. Midnight needed a bit more care and treatment, but her wound was completely healed three weeks later.

My cousin added a few tiger teeth and claws to Tank's necklace. He also hung a tooth and a claw of the tiger around Midnight's neck. At first she did not like the idea and tried to scratch off her necklace, but little by little she got used to it. The rest of the tiger's claws and teeth were distributed to ailing children in the hamlet, because according to old beliefs, tiger claws and teeth ward off the devils that make children sick.

Tank looked even more impressive with the tiger's claws and teeth added to his necklace. People stopped to watch him when he passed by, even though they had seen him many times before. The noise made by his necklace when he shook his head sounded much deeper and fuller now. As for the tiger's skin, we hung it in the sitting room, beside the hide of the wild hog.

After his successful fight against the tiger, Tank was relieved of his duty of tilling the soil during the rainy season. Other inhabitants of the hamlet let my father know that if his other buffaloes could not till all the land he owned, they would send theirs to help. Tank's duty now was to guard the herd in the pasture during the dry season or to carry me on his back during our joyful outings in the field or woods.

The Fallen Hero

B ut my pleasant outings with Tank
were not to last. War was spreading
through our country and even over
our little hamlet. One day fierce fighting
between the French forces and the Resis-
tance led by Ho Chi Minh erupted when I
was in the field tending the family herd. The
battle was so close that we tried to run away
and seek shelter in the nearby river. I rushed
Tank and the rest of the herd toward the

river, but suddenly I realized that Tank was lagging behind and limping. I went to him and saw that he had been hit. A stray bullet had pierced his chest.

With my urging he made it to the river, but he looked very weak when he lay down. I patted Tank's neck lightly to let him know that I was with him, and that he would be all right. I saw tears in his eyes, but I did not know whether he suffered from the wound or was sad because he knew he was going to die.

When the battle in the hamlet was over, Tank could not get up. He died only an hour later. We buried Tank in the graveyard where we buried all the dead of our family, and for the first time I saw my father cry. I thought about keeping the wild hog's tusks and the tiger's claws and teeth for myself, but then I changed my mind and placed them on Tank's grave.

Early the next morning I went to Tank's grave to burn incense for him. When my mother saw me crying, she came and stood by my side. I told her that only yesterday Tank had carried me on his back and walked toward the river on the little path. It just

didn't seem possible that he now lay underground. If the bullet had not hit him, Tank would have lived as long as old Water Jug. Tank *should* have lived as long as Water Jug. My mother reminded me that at least Tank had left behind a son, and that the calf looked as promising as his father had. She said that she would ask my father to give Tank's son to me, and then I could name the calf as I chose.

She suggested that we go to the rice field to give my father a surprise visit. But when we got to the field, I recognized Tank's footprints on many paths—they were much bigger than those of the other buffaloes. The sight of all the places where we had been together made me even more miserable. Seeing me crying again, my mother changed her mind and decided we should go home. I would have preferred to remain alone in the field, but she said that she wanted me to be with her. When she stooped to wipe my face, I saw tears in her eyes, too.

I could not sleep well for many nights after Tank's death. Often I got up and groped my way toward the window, and from there I could see Tank's grave. Sometimes it was covered with shadows when it rained on the small hamlet. But even on dark nights, once in a while lightning allowed me to catch a glimpse of his grave. In these brief shining moments I could see clearly the wild hog's tusks and the tiger's claws and teeth. Small tokens of the glory of the fallen hero.

The war would take many more, many precious things from me and my family, but none would carry the staggering shock of losing Tank. How could future losses surprise me now that I knew that a single misplaced bullet could destroy such a powerful creature, such a benevolent being, such a good friend?

Huynh Quang Nhuong

was born in Mytho, Vietnam. Upon being graduated from Saigon University with a degree in chemistry, he was drafted into the South Vietnamese army. Mr. Huynh was permanently paralyzed by a gunshot wound received on the battlefield, and in 1969 he came to the United States for additional medical treatment. He now makes his home in Columbia, Missouri.

Mr. Hyunh's first book for children, *The Land I Lost: Adventures of a Boy in Vietnam,* was published in five different languages and received many honors and awards. He is also the author of several published and produced plays based on Vietnamese legends and folklore. Mr. Hyunh received a Creative Writing Fellowship Grant from the National Endowment for the Arts in 1990.

Jean and Mou-sien Tseng

have illustrated many distinguished picture books, including *The Seven Chinese Brothers,* an ALA Notable Children's Book, and the Vietnamese folk tale *Why Ducks Sleep on One Leg.*

Mr. Tseng has also received the Golden Goblet Award for excellence in Chinese painting from the Art Society of China. The Tsengs are the artists for *A Treasury of Mermaids,* a HarperCollins Children's picture book.

The Tsengs have two grown daughters and live in Glen Cove, New York.

DATE DUE

FEB 1 0 2002			
NOV 3 0 2002			
JAN 1 9 2003			
MAY — 1 2003			
JUL 2 0 2004			
JUL 2 2 2008			
GAYLORD			PRINTED IN U.S.A.